Books by Howard Moss

POEMS
Notes from the Castle   1979
A Swim off the Rocks   1976
Buried City   1975
Selected Poems   1971
Second Nature   1968
Finding Them Lost   1965
A Winter Come, A Summer Gone   1960
A Swimmer in the Air   1957
The Toy Fair   1954
The Wound and the Weather   1946

CRITICISM
Writing Against Time   1969
The Magic Lantern of Marcel Proust   1962

EDITED, WITH AN INTRODUCTION
The Poet's Story   1973
The Nonsense Books of Edward Lear   1964
Keats   1959

SATIRE
Instant Lives   1974

Notes from the Castle

Notes from the Castle

Poems by Howard Moss

New York Atheneum *1979*

These poems have been published in the following magazines:

ANTAEUS: *Stars*
THE PARIS REVIEW: *News from the Border*
PARTISAN REVIEW: *The Research of Dancers*
THE NEW LEADER: *Have You Forgotten*
THE NEW YORKER: *Elegy for My Sister; Incomplete and Disputed
    Sonatas; At Georgica Beach; Four Birds; Notes from the Castle;
    Listening to Jazz on a Summer Terrace; At the Cafe; Standards;
    Aspects of Lilac; Gravel; Impatiens; A Fall; The Repetitions;
    The Sleeper; The Promissory Note; Many Senses: Mexico City;
    The Night Express; Remains; Rilke's Childhood; Torso*
    (Brodsky); *I Sit by the Window* (Brodsky)
THE NEW YORK REVIEW OF BOOKS: *The Long Island Night*
THE VANDERBILT REVIEW: *What the Heart Wants*

The versions of poems by Joseph Brodsky were made
for his book *A Part of Speech,* published by Farrar,
Straus & Giroux, *Torso* copyright © 1978 by Farrar,
Straus & Giroux, Inc.; *I Sit by the Window* copyright ©
1979 by Farrar, Straus & Giroux, Inc.

For Mary Mothersill *and* Harold Sanger

Contents

I

Gravel

I

The many here
Are like those crossing
Rivers into exile, the many felled
In Mexico by the crossbows of Cortes,
The French falling in the Russian snows,
But none like these are constantly run over
By heavy wheels or suddenly shadowed
By heights it is impossible to fathom.

The most gentle of the small stones
Has fallen in love
With the ordinary flower beds of summer
Lying helpless till winter effects
The divorce of sunlit wood and violet,
The slow parting of shadow and hydrangea.

Among these dead, these small leftover
Fragments of something once colossal—
The glacier moving southward with its ice—

There is one lying in the path in stillness,
One awaking to a grand piano
Somewhere in the house,
Who is grappling inside the hard room of its head
With syllables, or a phrase of song,
All ears gathering to sound.

2
If you should hear
The sound of the rustling
Of fallen oak leaves,
Would it remind you
Of the wind in the upright
Bole of summer?
And would the upright
Oak tree remember
The mast of the green sail
High above it?

High above
The level
Of gravel?

3
Suppose they were countries,
Territories,
Each with its central
Intelligence, each
With its nucleus
Surrounded by matter,
And spilled from the flatbed
Of a truck
Onto a roadway,
Or hauled to a roof,
Afraid of nothing but tar.

4
They have laid down
The armor of the big stone
By being movable,
Their lichen and moss
Rubbed to nothing
By endless stormy
Crack divisions.

Today they are hit
By a steady rain;
Rivulets run
Between, connecting
The white and the brown one,
The gray and the blue one.

5
There is a line downtown
Which is the end of Italian ices

And the beginning of trading posts
In Chinatown. Not as definite

As edges that separate small stones,
It is unquestionably there,

There in a park where old men weigh
The Chinese young on trays of swing.

6

A foot at wrong angles
Shoots one under
The house
Into permanent black,

A hand flings one
Onto a field
Into the desert
Of sun forever.

7

To the ant
They are possibly boulders,

To the hawk
Nothing at all.

To themselves
They are always a mixture

Never to be singled
Out as one—

They yearn
To be made separate

Or to be part
Of some great thing.

They yearn
To be made solid.

8

These pebbles bristle. Whoever loves
The feel of nails could bed here forever
Stuck by the sharpest prickles of needles,
The flat blade and the serrated edge,
The pointed end, the ridges of hardness
Pressing in and hurting slightly
To stick in the sweating flesh of summer
Till somebody mad for a coldsuit of water
Might lie in the heat of an August driveway
Covered from head to foot with gravel,
Rolling this way and that in a fever.

9

Bone of a leaf
On stone,

You are the smallest
Lithograph.

10

Whatever has been taken out
Will be put back,
The drawers filled again
With their pressed clothes,
The organs of the body

Folded back whole,
And the shell underfoot,
Inadvertently broken,
Reassembled
With every flute of the scallop
Intact, and be placed
In its place in the glass
Container, and
The wings of the moth
Singed so the body
Spiralled in flame
Will arise anew
To be healed again,
To achieve again
Its rise and fall,

So the name of the thing
Will be truly the thing,
And stone
Will be more than stone.

Z Thu 21 Nov 1996 11:27AM Item(s)
checked out to Chenier, Deanna Ir
ne.

TITLE
BARCODE   DUEDATE
sychological aspects of pregnancy,
bi 31888005369021   02 Jan 1997

lotes from the castle : poems / by
low 31888007777494   02 Jan 1997

II

Notes from the Castle

The sunlight was not our concern or even
The pane it shone through, and no one was going
Down for the mail, and the four lettuces
The gardener brought as a gift seemed to be
A calculated bounty, so that early on
We knew we were going to be stuck with ourselves
The rest of the day, the vicissitudes
Marching in rows from the forest, the balms
Not arriving till nightfall. On the prowl
Since morning, the wind had a touch too much
Of motivation, an annoying way
Of exactly ruffling the same oak leaf
As if it were practicing a piano trill;
All day, repetitive birds, far off,
Were either boring themselves to death
Or, drunk on instinct, doing their thing:
Ritual dances, territorial rites—
The whole imperial egg. What nests
Ambition is weaving in us is hard
To say: after the flat occasion,
The unshared sphere, each childish wish
Grows hopeless finding this is what the world is.
For this, the recommended cures are useless:
A cheery hello to the disaffected
At breakfast? A soupful of tears at dinner?
You could spill the whole silly story out
To one more demanding, ill-tempered beauty
You happened to meet at the A. & P.,
And still every greedy shopping cart,

First overstuffed and then abandoned
In the parking lot, would leave in its wake
Some human need, ignored, half-starved . . .
Torn between having nothing to say
And saying it, whole diaries get down:
How terrible to have dressed beautifully for the rain! . . .
I was launched on New York's bisexual muddle . . .
And so on. And always the hoped-for redeemer
Turns up and turns with a country stare:
The girl in the lime linen shorts, the boy
With blond corn-silk tow hair, the heart
Speeding up until they speak: the dross
Of cars, the sportsman's life, and money;
And so, believing that you had come
To rest among the innocent soldiers
Of sleep, you had merely stumbled on
Another temporary battlefield
As never-lasting as the shine of water.

The Night Express

That moment we neared the reservoir
Dry wit dried up aware that water
Was no longer there for the taking. Hazel
And birch, those secret, solitary drinkers,
Were suddenly duplicated everywhere,
Even the ground consuming its potion.
The word on every lip was "parched."
Could the desert be a stone's throw away,
As so many people had guessed? In her bath,
The old lady down the road was appalled
To find herself knee-deep in rust,
This after years of a limpid clearness,
Soap beautifully wrapped and scented—
It was better than a sojourn at a thousand spas.
The sodas of the springs, the dew
Knew they were doomed not to be, feather-
Bedders of a union that had seen its day.
And so moisture, morning mist, and streaks
Of rain became so valuable collectors
Held out cans especially designed
To catch every drop of the cold sweat
Of the night express as it went roaring by.

The Sleeper

Did you mark me, or I mark you,
Ambiguous hunter, gentle sleeper,
As, toward the bull's eye where we race,
The sunny become the men of winter?

Those tears that were the mead of snow—
Snow fences, leggings, masks of breath—
Are floating off toward the bluing hills
Somewhere in memory to the left,

Past where the mind has put down now
Its single husk in the long row,
While in the mirror's face the storm
Rattles its foil for the last time.

News from the Border

The fishermen lug in their nets, the take's
Too small, the natural's shunted aside
For derricks busy recouping the wastes
Of the limitless profits of coal and oil.
Barely able to reach the dunes
(The other half of the parenthesis
In reverse), the waves have had years of going
On like this. As blue as gas,
The sea lights up, goes out. The breakers
Pursue a few mad screaming gulls,
Mean little beasts hooked on garbage.

And further along, there's the hotel's
Honeycomb windows looking out to sea,
A tray of ice-cubes, each with its sniper.
Yet the summer clients stay faithful:
For instance, in Room 608,
Ms. Minerva, a former goddess, is keen
On not getting up. "One day," she threatens,
"Is so like another that one will come
When I won't even try at all. Brandy?"

But others are dying like Florida love-bugs
On beaches so covered with freighter fat
That even birds evolutionally adjusted
To the profit motive are saying, "We can't
Take it anymore." In South America,
An orchid enthusiast has stupidly mated
A gentle species in love with itself

With a waxy, dumb, hysterical affair,
Whose volunteers will cover the country,
Approach the border, then march across it,
And before you can say, "Muchas gracias, señor,"
Destroy what is left of civilization.

At the Café

At the café, at an outdoor table
Fronting the last of the puppet shows,
We have come to sip a bit of brandy
And watch the rapidly descending evening.
Violinists scrape the bow of air,
Arguments begin and finish soon,
As if philosophy were running a café
Where nothing is served but old ideas;
Tensed against the wine-soaked washrag
Of the sky the trees erect themselves
In the last small oblivion of lights;
Talk grows animated . . . someone screams . . .
This passes, these days, for the Bohemian.
Still, the knees of two bright things
Are touching . . . Everyone's lost the theme:
What is the mind compared to it,
To feeling's theatre always in flames,
On the stage, its aging, ludicrous opera
Still faintly heard among the ruins?

The Research of Dancers

The dancer's leg stops in mid-air.
The library researcher looking up
Something or other in the catalogue
Decides to take a five-minute breather.
He walks out past a famous painting.
Meanwhile, elsewhere, things are getting done:
The snow is kept from falling through nets
At an Aero-Biotic Arctic Station,
A fish is taught breathing at Yale . . .

Can countries be scrapped in favor of people?

How sure are the dance floors under the dancers
When it's heavy going in an arabesque?
How grimy are the nails of the librarian
Always a hairsbreadth away from genius?
You'd think they'd come clean, turn white from awe.

Are thoroughbred horses being born somewhere
Ready to be harnessed for their final races?

The dancer's foot has been suspended too long;
He longs for a resolution—an ending.
And the librarian's data must be done by dusk—
He, too, has a serious place to go home to.

For the dead, taps and reveille are one.

As the dancer places a tentative foot
On the floor of the stage, it rises to meet it,

The inanimate everywhere shudders awake,
The library stacks have just been struck
With their first good idea for a book in years;
Outside, the straw is dreaming of bricks,
As if it, too, had been activated
By beautiful, personal, spontaneous forms.

Have You Forgotten

Have you forgotten the sweetness of women,
Their treble cries, the underworld of milk?
How in the fleshy inside of an elbow
The warm hollow trembles with blue silk—
All luscious opaque roundness in a blur
Of bedroom coverlet, of rind and mound,
Those supple thighs I nested in at twelve
Whose milk-white forms melted the horizon's
Aggregate of birds into empty distance.

To walk by heavy mirrors of a myth
With the greedy mouth everyone begins with
And feed on nothing but the self reflected
Is to know how pleasure ceases, does away with
Savor, and the attributes of Eden
End up in a darkroom of details,
Or a day of too much light whose sun erases
Privacies gone flat, communication
A letter bomb arriving in the mails.

The Repetitions

For Robert Nunnelley and Gerald Coble

All this loose activity: the quick-
Silver fish alive in the Battenville stream;
The blaze of the sedentary copper pot
In the kitchen; cats' eyes; the afternoon
Canyon of a street gone dead, and then,
Maximum New York electrified
At night; the snow falling in a park
I walked through once to the brim of a world
Unseen but guessed at: the treacherous crevasse—
Tall trees, steady light, unsteady wind.

What fool would want the past, its rooms'
Worn lintels, windows silted by dust?
They appear again in daydream or dream:
Corridors, alcoves, the vaultings of just
Apprehendable living rooms . . . space, and the stars
Theatrically lowered on an autumn night
So the breath is caught in a limitless net
Of branches stretching toward another house,
Where a stranger is watching a lighted screen,
His hand fallen over the edge of a couch.

I walk down the slope to the river again;
On the bank, dry leaves, their poisonous flags
Withered in birth by the chemical breath
Of the paper factory reopened downstream.
Motionless, shadowy, under a rock,

Trout hang for protection. Boy scouts of the sun,
We took the old rowboat through rapids of froth
And found the lost cache of broken marble
Not far from the abandoned tracks; now long
Slabs of it tiered like railroad ties
Make up your graduated terrace steps.

Wan, thin willows color themselves in;
Forsythia branches burgeon and thicken;
Invisible, barely heard music—the lots'
First hammers announce the arrival of spring:
They come back the unrealness of time, of age,
Repeated obsessions, repeated loves,
They live, they live, as if they had never been.

III

Many Senses: Mexico City

For Clyde Miller

I
No light. Think of living in a stone.
Then flying zigzag through cardboard scenery
Changing into loopholes for a plane
Diving straight into a bowl of mountains
Whose hollow thickens to a modest plain
Bounded by the rolltop hills . . .

In grammar school, Q-Tips dipped in glue
Attached transparent capsules filled with coal
And silver (foil) and tin onto
The wrinkled (Kleenex) hills

                                    that rise above
What now appears . . . is that Tenochtitlán?

It sends a shiver down my spine.
I look it up:
columna vertebral . . .

We spent an afternoon smoothing out a valley
Smeared with a rubberized fine skin of clay
That tightened, drying . . .

Tighter than the window seat I'm in?

The ground is rising up to meet . . . We're down.

2

These primitive faces tell you nothing,
Having floated off their museum pedestals,
The plazas and the courtyards filling up
With evening statuary, street after street
Named for rivers, and the rivers flowing . . .
The Mexican lesson: learning how to wait . . .
In the Zona Rosa—
Madison Avenue turned into a maze—
The colored pinprick of a traffic light
Needles through the smog . . .

Never have so many hurried to be late.

3

Americans clog the aisles at Sanborn's.
It's impossible to find a postage stamp.
"Not today, señor. *Nada. Nada.*"
High above, a sign: "Racine Hydraulics."
Another: "Sanatorio del Puente,"
Wittily translated by my friend as "Clean
By the Bridge." In fact, it is a hospital . . .

4

Architecture? Washington and Paris.
Mosaic-Colonial-Imperial-Gaudí.
And then a vast Los Angeles of slums.

There is a tenement. There a Sheraton.

What does the fly care for the web's design?

5
The city's sinking.

Half the street's an inch or so below
The other half, so that your shoulders go
Slantwise. Bilateral symmetry, amigo,

¿ *Dónde está* ? The sidewalk's cracked
Along the mortar between the tiles
A fissure like an earthquake's breakage line.

6
Somehow earth—or is it dirt? or dust?—
Takes on a special meaning: death in life;
Even the flour made of corn that rolls
Everything edible into its thin tortilla
Suggests rubbed stone, the hard, deft hand,
The graze of flesh on stone, whose dust will make
New flesh to turn to stone, the flesh
To corn . . .

7
At the Anthropology Museum
The fountain is the tallest mushroom in the world,
Its underside a circle of ribbed flints
Pleated tight, its razor blades of rain
Dropping toward the sidewalk sieve below
To open into showers, into spray . . .

8

Limes. Silver-papered chocolates. Straw.
Someone in a park who longs to be
More than a friend and less than a lover,
Whose eyes go dim among the fireflies . . .

9

The weather's delicate crisps, the clouds'
Martyred effulgence, about to say
Something immortal, hurry away
To state the temporary state of truth
And find even that impossible to say . . .

"It rains a little, señor, every day."

In the hotel garden,
Could that be
Marimbas in the distance,
The auto-shine
Of a Volkswagen Beetle idling by,
A sort of Spanish-Moorish tile design
Reflected in its polished hood, the shine—
Even though it shines like any shine—

Sleepy with no news, the radio on,
Going by . . . and gone?

Autographs and animals, vines and twigs,
A net of scrambled shadow finely drawn
On the tablecloth,
On civilized food no hunter kills for,

No fisherman risks the salty rocks for,
And yet the primitive is there in the corner,
There where the shadows pile up into rock . . .

Thickening with sleep, the afternoon . . .

We circle round to three o'clock's dead stop.

10
Think of the Renaissance rising out of blood,
A baroque angel shedding tears above
A human sacrifice, hearts torn out alive,

Fear at the steps, and under the stone knife
The steep steps leading up a flattened cone
To the altar at the top, the fearful priests . . .

And what this city teems with life for,
Like any city, is a city's dream:
The management of comfort, if not here,
Then up in heaven, the plumed serpent
And the smoking mirror converted to
Some Catholic version of the rites of spring.

11
We leave as we began: Airport-Airport.
In the plane at last, I close my eyes.
Carlotta walks into the Vatican;
Kneeling to kiss the Papal ring, she lifts
Her streaming, insane face to him,
Her cheekbones sanding into Aztec stone.

IV

The Long Island Night

Nothing as miserable has happened before.
The Long Island night has refused its moon.
La belle dame sans merci's next door.
The Prince of Darkness is on the phone.

Certain famous phrases of our time
Have taken on the glitter of poems,
Like "Catch me before I kill again,"
And "Why are you sitting in the dark alone?"

Listening to Jazz
on a Summer Terrace

The stars come out. They might be made of snow.
Below, a subtle drumbeat slips and snares
Its honey and sandpaper into nerves
That pull long shadows out of paper bags
Or shift like gears behind the window shades:
Ozone-sweat on chromium, green felt
Saliva stops, the shifty seeds of drums,
That flimsy shimmy, that old rat-a-tat!
Ampules of musk and dust geraniums!

At Georgica Beach

How roughly ambivalent the seizure is
Of the sea to fix each wave it undoes
In the wake each time of the breakage it was,

Each coming in to the edge of drydock,
And then, underneath, the long drawing back,
Leaving the minor clatter of shellshock . . .

It's day. The wind's up. The ocean's gambling
With light. The dice thrown, the game is running
Away with itself in runnels and creases—

The long cliff-hangers, just as they strengthen
Their hold on the surface, break and capsize
Into the sinking spools and renewals

Of things getting ready only to be things.

Remains

Long after the liner has been put in drydock
The wish still steers the rudder of its will.
They are carting away the remains of a novel
Two people worked on for years. In a park,
Old-timers watch the spring leaves re-hanging
Their bits and pieces. Someone else, far away,
Through vertical skyscraper windows sees
The street being swept of its autumn leaves.

Rilke's Childhood

What angel woke
one morning in his blood
while he stood standing
in a childhood dream,
the lake of a mirror
in the bedroom before him?
Or at the breakfast table
saw in the cold milk
winter going by,
out the window a slow train
silently drawn across
a field of ice,
the suspended breath
of mourners in the air,
the ponds darkening
below a line of trees?

The Promissory Note

Promissory note
Of the stirred life,
Tonight I opened
The rare book of you

And found
The last page missing.
It is six o'clock,
And you still owe me

Everything.

V

Elegy for My Sister

1

Getting out of bed one day, you broke
Your leg simply by standing up,
The bones too frail, the marrow gone,
Melted into a kind of eggshell sawdust,
The Crab, and chemotherapy against it,
The cure as killing as the pain it cured . . .

Why torture myself? Or you?—sailed into
The port of Nothing or that Elysium
Of childish happiness the heart sets store by,
Which, for you, would be a house in Larchmont,
Or the first time you arrived in Paris. . . .

2

Now the vials have closed and all the druggists
Vanished into smoke, along what walks
Will the ghost of you appear in a summer nightgown,
Silvery as moonlight on a sill,
Supple as the girl you were, who, frowning,
Dazzled guests with showy piano pieces?
You never got the hang of it, never quite took in
The Bach Partitas or the Chopin Études,
Languishing always over "Clair de Lune"—
Moony on the upstairs porch and downcast,
Waiting for the phone to ring, or waiting
Simply for the end of waiting. Left in
My possession—the irony of phrases!—
Is a photograph of you posed on a pony
Somewhere in Maine—white cap, white coat—

And one from Lakewood. I remember going
Up by train once, dancing in the aisles
While the train sneaked through faint zebra woods of
    pine. . . .

3
That afternoon will come when the schoolgirl walking
Home from the classroom in the spring will feel
The first onslaught of the terror of seasons,
The blood of the hour a permanent imprint.
Approaching the bridge, will she be in her newness
The last straw just as the ship in the river

Appears and the jaws of the bridge fly open—
The drab barge below with its scruffy captain
Commanding the air with bleatings and whistles,
The smokestack's blunt, swift-moving cigar
Blurring the trees in a smudge of smoke,
The birds in the sky in a net, then not?

Above the run-down, oily garages
Of the Bronx—old brickwork, carwash rinses,
The abandoned piecemeal junk of the car lots—
A vapor trail goes into the workshop
Of the clouds, the spring comes on in the bushes,
Forsythia making its annual statement.

The bridge underneath is ever so slightly
Tearing a suture of itself in secret;
And what is most feared is about to happen:

The stage-set of a world taken for granted
Will drop from the sky, robots of ashes
In clouds grow solidly real, and murders

That always before occurred at a distance
Strangle the neck at home. How the small thing
Matters: the phones getting through, the cables
Never exhaling invisible, lethal
Fumes, the macadam keeping its bubbles
Of tar intact. . . . The bridge sways, opens,

And the cell is about to distort the message
Life had meant it to carry from the start,
Letting death's emperor through. The tiny
Deadly protein blossoms. The blossoms
Open to yellow, true yellow in the spring
Outside your Memorial Hospital window.

4
What errors you made you made in wanting
To be warm again or held or human
And not for the wolf of cash or the mean,
Sloe-eyed beauty of power or the game
Of the wily outwitting the unaware,
Or simulated pain used as a lure.
How stupid the endings of life can be!
Old age not seeing the sea at its foot,
Not hearing the music still to be heard.
Dead to all things but the shape of the self,
The violent tear out blood with their hands,

The insane hold up the cardboard pieces
Of a world they can no longer fit together,
And the cruel: the slack nurse, the greedy aide,
The doctor no longer aware of pain . . .

5
How all the terminals of the body
Ply their invisible servings and turnings,
The loading of freight, the slipping of cargo

Into the cell, the interior vision
Blind as the blood erasing the causeway
Connecting vital island to island.

What are ideas but architecture
Taking nature to heart and sustaining
Inviolable forms: the fleur-de-lis,

The subtle acanthus, the shell-like dominions
Of diamond accretions royal on coal,
The Gothic tower and the rabbit warren,

The fine interchange of matter and matter,
The natural and social shifting in the bonds
Of dialogues and elegies that rise from soil.

6
All the allowable days on circling
Boats turning inward toward the center
Of the circle of the water of the river

Have been disallowed by the squarely arriving
Tugboat from which a peg-legged captain
Smoking a panatela is lowered
Into a launch behind him his shadowy
Crew and now you see them advancing
Climbing the ropes toward the deck you're on
The smoke the river the trees going past you
Into the mist the birds growing weaker
Downriver somewhere there is connected
Song water falling rapids of birdcalls
Way off the cry of the throat of fever
The faintest releases of animal sound
The sky coming nearer, closer and closer,
The distances moving toward you and farther
Away the repeated echoes of names
Called across water   then it is over.

VI

Aspects of Lilac

By the turn of the driveway, two lilacs have called
Attention to themselves, not by an excess
Of bloom but by an attenuation
Of design: altered shadow on gravel.
Gone for good are those understated
Cases I rescued from worthless soil:
Ripped-off dusty miller from the beach,
Or, struck by overdoses of rain,
Spoiled spotted-leaf geranium. Worse
Is the thud of birds that kill themselves
By flinging their bodies with force against
Glass windows and doors as if this were
Some sort of morgue for feathered things.
The deaf and dumb would find all language
Futile here; nature is silent—
But underneath the silence, struggle.
While powder-puff clouds are showing off
Quickening shapes against more stately
Clouds behind them, an ant has dragged
A fly across the threshold, a mealy
Bug fastened its sticky jaws
Into the crotch of two green stems,
Chewing the asparagus fern to scruff.
Last night the moon had a Byzantine flare
Of lemon gold like the goldleaf halos
One sees in the early Italian masters—
Venice, in fact, comes to mind, the palazzos'
Sandcastle, ice-cream feats, effects
Childish but pleasing, of spun-stone heights,
While a rat stands gnawing a lettuce leaf

At the edge of one of the canals. And sex
Like a frog jumps onto the screen at once,
Its spiritual and degraded aspects
Equally keen. In fall, when the first
Earth colors harden and oak fire starts
Its flame and rust, memory dotes
On the old clichés of the unexpected.
Desire never knows the end of the book
Any more than the leaves of the lilac dug
Up in the woods, brought home, and planted
Can tell us whether its roots next spring
Will burst into purple or white cascades.

Four Birds

"Wake to the sun," the rooster croaked,
First bird of the day. The world, light-flecked,
Chiselled its lineaments into form.
Where was all that fine light coming from?

"Trance at the wonder," the second sang,
Whose five dry notes urged the ongoing
Afternoon on. "Why wake and stir?"
It asked. And asked. There was no answer.

"Live through the muddle." That from the next one.
Not very helpful. It looked like rain,
Or fog in the offing. Twilight. Then
It sang again from an oak or pine.

Silence. How I waited for the fourth!
Time was a negative dipped into its bath,
The dark a fixative that slowly made
For every windowpane its window shade.

No messages arrived. No music bared
The soul for its penitence. Up the stairs
No hint of a footfall. The night passed.
"Croak by your hand," said the crow at last.

Incomplete and Disputed Sonatas

1
After the plagues and the dispossessions,
Survival's one idea gives way
To ideas of civility:
Immigrants rise out of muddy shoes
Up to their sky-high penthouse suites,
A piano waxed to perfection wheels
On all three legs down a pine-needle path
Through woods. French windows reveal the sky,
And one sharp branch of forsythia
Sticks its yellow muzzle of a gun
Into the proper corner window,
Making the composition perfect.

2
Someone playing Schumann begins
To alter the prepared arrangements—
The idea of dissolution comes back again:
The needle's track runs backward in its grooves,
A window-cleaner like a flake of icing
Drops to the ground, the glass shatters,
Cutting badly on the way down.

3
Still,
You may see, curled up in still
Another window,
A girl intent on reading a novel,
Her hair suffused with sunlight blonder
Than she. Music by Mozart,

The G-Minor Quintet saying
How nothing lasts
But music by Mozart.

4
Are we approaching the coast?
Dark, you have given too many assignments.
Rain drums on the slattings of the deck.
Cold warns the room of its sudden menace.

5
Wagnerian sails
Go by the window—
Somewhere in fog a net and trident,
Neptune stranded on a tip of pine,
Appalled to be a god in a suburb.

6
Every day to wake to the world's work,
To take apart the watchwork of seasons,
Houses I cannot remember, palaces
Burning among the ghostly senators,
Or around a fire a circle of men,
The dogs with their wary eyes walking
Out of the forest to become domestic . . .
Tonight the storm's electrical transformers,
The purring abusiveness of cats in love.

7
Lately among apparently leafless
Trees I have had these afternoons
Of solitude and of loneliness,
As if I might die before I could tell
Those whom I loved that I had loved them,
As if when I woke I would slowly walk
To a bay window, look down, and see
Myself lying lifeless on gravel.

What the Heart Wants

For R. P. W.

Happiness: what the heart wants . . .
ROBERT PENN WARREN

How peace surprises us in August!
This sudden awareness of happiness
Comes, I think, from the sun on water,

Or maybe that flurry on the banister
When the light allowed its print to form there,
Allowed for anything to be imagined.

Yet outside, imagination founders:
Ants bringing in the relief of extras,
Sex's short pajamas on the line—

Intensely ludicrous that one cartoon
Of spirit dallying with earthly matter,
But not for long. We want each other

To arrive in cars on cleanswept gravel,
Separate but equal, poem and novel
Read but not memorized, the mind at double

Before the sunset's colored slides above
The telephone wires will be ending as
A distant conflagration seen through woods.

Impatiens

Your current pain no longer divides you
From the world of pain, bringing with it
Impatiens—pots of it, pink, red, white,
Plants glimpsed on a sill. Your pain
Lessens not by division but fattens
On earlier pain, those filaments and dredges
And tons of sand bottomed in a bag,
Sunsets staged in the curves of chairs,
Penitent clouds that do not argue
With the best intentions, and friends who desire
Both your health and the destruction of it,
Who love you, but love your pain as well.

There are those who have traced its trace on air;
Walking across their territories like kings,
They have sensed imperial gore somewhere,
Across the seas or beyond the mountains,
Staking out new sites, endlessly repeating
The warrior's success, colonies and tracts,
Landfalls, and even the ruin of grandeur
Beheld one night in an English dream.

Your pain is crossing the borders of patience,
Worse at night in a hospital room
Plastered with the cries of those who died there.

Your pain. It is intolerable. It is
Hardly though the anguish of the tortured
Beaten on cement, sleepless, raving,
Fingernails ripped out by skillful priests,
The grim surgeons who enjoy inflicting
The international instruments of torment,
The rack, restraints, electric currents,
Truncheons, all ready there for use,
For the vomit, urine, and feces of the cell.
So in all ways you are illustrated
And diminished, though you suffer at the sight
Of a small clay pot of thriving impatiens,
Pink, because it reminds you of someone,
A child waking up to the terror of love.

A Fall

A sadness now has entered into it,
Our love affair this autumn of the glooms,
Our unenlightened, dumb, unstated marriage—
Your eyes and silence. My gift of tongues.

Taste glosses you in its great mirror.
I wander among the distributed notes
Of the leaves. Are the birds art critics?
New canvases drive them out of their wits.

Those that are left. They're mostly gone,
The birds *and* the canvases. The geese
Having deployed in V's, the trees
Naked among a million oak leaves.

On island nights, the dark was never dark
Enough, the stars too bright. A kerosene
Aladdin lamp threw shadows on the screen.
You turned it down. And other lights went on.

Standards

Sadly among the patient standards
Of trees the twirlers arrive to conduct
The last of the summer's orchestral pieces.
The garden's icetray of seeds is about
To swing back into its glacial room;
In less and less tree, in more and more shades,
Being is only a caster of rings,
A moment loaned by an Indian giver
Each year becoming more subtle in taking
Down the last partitions of leaves.

Across the field, in a field, some horses
Chomp on summer, green crop turning
Into a lawn of lap robes skillfully
Stitched, moss mounds thinning to moons
Of suède—so they appear from a distance.
The air is a brandy snifter of pine,
Fresh in this land of oaks and azaleas,
Of acid earth rhododendrons love,
A bit too sandy for roses but
Perfect for lilies that last a day.

The butterfly's parturition, its swift
Demise occur in a wink, and things
That took their own sweet time to be
Themselves reluctantly take their leave:
Seeds, weeds, the gods of the seasons
Bowing in mist, while in the wings
Two sets of actors are exchanging costumes,
The street urchins shaking hands with the angels,
The woods about to speak to the axeman.

Two times the light gets lacier: when
Insects pattern the leaves with bites,
A ferocious munching one hears at night
In spring—an invasion of gypsy moths—
And now, when the leaves are no longer partial
But slip away and are totally gone,
So though there is less and less of light,
Still, by being able to shine
Down through the vertical hallways of oaks,
It seems to increase in intensity.

The seeds with their little valises fly
Over the scene and look for a landing;
Any spot of common earth will do
In the sun. Preferably moist. The dew
Does wonders. Already one sees next year
Spring up: tree, flower, bush, and weed,
The butterfly conjoin with the tiger lily,
The roadside aster purple the border,
The process random, none of it wary,
Forgetting how dumb form is in history.

Ocean houses breaded with lilac,
A dry stick of a hut embedded in sand,
Things man-made and some things natural
Go: one storm slams through a solid
Wall, brings trees to their knees, and sucks
A beach house down from the dunes in boards;
The beach changes its contours nightly,
And so, if you are coming to see me,
Come soon. Today's astringent, perfect,
A perfection not to be known for long.

VII

Stars

For James Merrill

In some versions of the universe the stars
Race through their orbits only to arrive
Back where they started from, like me planning to
Visit you in Greece—how many times?—I never have,
And so your house in Athens still remains
A distinct possibility, like one the stars
Foretell in the sky or spell out on the magic
Ouija board you use to bring to life,
Out of the night's metaphysical static,
Ephraim, that Greek, first-century Jew
Who telegraphs his witty messages to you,
The cup as pointer capturing alive
The shorthand of the occult, divinely comic . . .
But who's responsible for the result—
The spirit world or you?

                   Do you as I do
Have to fend off Freud's family reunions:
Those quadraphonic old familiar quartets
Positioned nightly, bored, around the bed—
No speaking parts, and two of them at least
Certified deadheads? What does friendship mean
Unless it is unchanging, unlike Ovid's
Metamorphoses where everyone's becoming
Something else—Poor Echo and her voice!
And poor unlistening, unhinged Narcissus;
Poised above the water for the glassy foreplay,
He sees more than himself in the reflecting pool:
It's Algol, the ecliptic—a variable.

We met in the forties (hard to believe—
You were in uniform and I in mufti.—)
And went our separate ways: you to matinées
At the Opera and I to the City Ballet.
Though one extraordinary day, much later,
We heard "Wozzeck" at a dress rehearsal,
Sitting in the empty Met at 39th Street
In a center box—was it Mrs. Morgan's?
(How much more pertinent to this poem's theme
If it had belonged to Mrs. Astor!)
The nascent glitter of the oval boxes,
Brass railings sheathed in velvet, dimming lights
Preparing the round hush for music's entrance,
The subtle musk of perfumed dust, and dusky
Presences, now ghosts, floating round the room
(Now itself a ghost, long since torn down):
Old opera stars and their old audiences.
What a performance! Never interrupted
Once by—God!—was it Mitropoulos?
I think it was. Another Greek. You know
How memory fuzzes up the facts. But one
Odd fragment still remains. You brought along
A paper bag with chicken sandwiches
We ate out in the lobby in the intermissions,
And never was a sandwich so delicious—
Drunk on music, we staggered down the stairs
To daylight streaming in to air the lobby,
Surprised to see—beyond the doors—Broadway!

Loew's "Valencia" 's ceiling made of stars
Was not "The Starlight Roof"—that came later—
Starry-eyed, I watched the North Star rise
At Fire Island Pines. Below the equator,
I assumed it *fell*, and the Dipper, in reverse,
Spilled the velvet black back into darkness—
All wrong, of course. At the Planetarium,
Projected stars I craned my neck to see
Brought back the "Valencia" 's vaudeville to me,
A passion of my childhood: backbend writhers,
Lariat rope-skippers, and a stream of comic
Yodellers from Switzerland who did their stuff
Under twinkling stars. Like these above:

Calculating Leda floats above the hedges
To surprise The Swan nightly at his pool
Opal in the moonlight as he drinks his fill,
Galaxies flung at random in the till
Of the Great Cash Register the world comes down to;
When the drawer slams shut, a once and only
Big Bang Theory may be shot to hell,
And not again the great unknown designer
Fling into the firmament the shining things
Above a world grown ludicrous or tragic,
And our sick century may not recover:
The Spanish War. The Yellow Star. Vietnam.
Five . . . or is it ten by now ? . . . assassinations.
The stars were crossed, the lifelines cut too soon—
And smaller fallings-off fall every day

Worse for being seen against the view
Of the starlight's inexhaustible display
Of which we cannot make out half the meaning . . .
Did Starbuck, on his watch, stare to starboard,
Gazing at the sea through meteoric showers,
And hear, above, the music of the spheres?
Or merely hear the watch bells chime the hours?

The Little Dipper in East Hampton dips
Above the pines, as if, at my fingertips,
Light so highly born could be borne down
From vibrancies that glisten and touch ground . . .
It brings the dawn, it brings the morning in.
I'm having coffee and reading your "Divine
Comedies." At "D": "*Dramatis Personae* . . .
Deren, Maya . . ." Maya and I once met
In Washington Square and talked for hours
Of images. Was film sheer poetry? Etcet.
Of "Meshes of the Afternoon," "At Land" . . .
I saw myself in both films recently . . .
How much I had forgot! My part's half cut . . .
I dazzled myself, though, just by being young.
And "Auden, Wystan," master star of all,
A major figure in the "Comedies,"
Poured wine for me at Cherry Grove and said
At least ten brilliant things too fast to hear—
Part wit, part stammer, part schoolboy pioneer,
His high-Church, camp, austere "My dear,"
Soon switched into the beach vernacular.
I've found that conversations with the great

Are almost invariably second-rate,
Yet, when he died, I felt that truth had left
The world for good, its foremost spokesman gone.
You meet the characters in Proust at parties,
Dimly aware that you are one yourself
Fated to be translated badly like
A comedy of manners curried into Greek
With too many stars, none self-effacing,
Or worse, find yourself dressed for a Fable,
Lightly disguised as the Star of Ages . . .
Saying that, I feel the slightest pull . . .
How odd! I think I'm drifting . . . Lifted up
Past houses, trees . . . And going up and up . . .
You're rising, too, into the stellar soup . . .
Stop! Where's Newton! Where is *gravity*?

In observation cars, beneath balloons,
We falter, float into the atmosphere
Of Webster's Third . . . or is it the O.E.D.?—
Either is outer space for you and me—
And soar aloft among word constellations.
The stars are verbs; the nouns are nova; pale
Adjectives grow bold at our approach;
The sulphur schools of fish are lit, and flare;
Paper fire-cinders feather into blackness
Their ember-edged remains, and then, no matter;
From your little lip of balcony you fish
Into the icy wastes; I cast my line
Into the squirming lists. Out of the blackened blue,
Racing upward into the stratosphere,

The purest draft of crystal veers toward you.
We sidle up through drop-cloths rushing down,
Go zigzag, pause, and coasting on a calm,
Reach up to pluck the stars like words to make
A line, a phrase, a stanza, a whole poem.
A planet's surface blinds us; we look down:
Moonlight's aluminum coats the molten wells . . .
Is that a comma? Or a quarter moon?
One decimal of saturated gold,
A coin drops in its slot, and turns to ash.
You scud into a diamond bed ahead,
I drop toward burning coals that soon grow cool . . .
Exclamation marks against the sky,
Our hanging baskets periods below,
We sway, like ski-lifts hung from chains. The dark
Is filled with phosphorescent question marks.
In a snow shuttle, the Great Bear flies,
Angling for the Pole. How light his fur!
The Dog Star puts his solar collar on.
It's crystal-cold. One needs the inner darkness
Lit by spirit lamps or, like Aladdin's,
Rubbed to bring the genie, warmth, back home.
Stupendous flocks . . . Is it the world in flames?
Or just the Milky Way? Too late! Too late!
Again we rise up through the lit bazaars,
Punchdrunk, against the carbon, seeing stars.

VIII Versions of Two Poems by Joseph Brodsky

Torso

If suddenly you walk on grass turned stone
and think its marble handsomer than green,
or see at play a nymph and faun that seem
happier in bronze than in any dream,
let your walking stick fall from your weary hand,
        you're in The Empire, friend.

Air, fire, water, fauns, naiads, lions
drawn from nature, or bodied in imagination,
everything God ventured and reason grew bored
nourishing have in stone and metal been restored.
This is the end of things. This is, at the road's end,
        a mirror by which to enter.

Stand in a niche, roll your eyes up, and watch
the ages vanish round the bend, and watch
how moss develops in the statue's groin,
how dust rains on the shoulders—that tan of time.
Someone breaks an arm off, and the head from the shoulders
        falls with the thud of boulders.

The torso left is a nameless sum of muscle.
In a thousand years a mouse, living in a hole,
with a claw broken off from trying to eke
a life out of granite, will scurry with a squeak
across the road one night and not come back to its burrow
        at midnight tonight. Or at daybreak tomorrow.

I Sit by the Window

I said fate plays a game without a score,
And who needs fish if you've got caviar?
The triumph of the Gothic style would come to pass
And turn you on—no need for coke, or grass.
    I sit by the window. Outside, an aspen.
    When I loved, I loved deeply. It wasn't often.

I said the forest's only part of a tree.
Who needs the whole girl if you've got her knee?
Sick of the dust raised by the modern era,
The Russian eye would rest on an Estonian spire.
    I sit by the window. The dishes are done.
    I was happy here. But I won't be again.

I wrote: The bulb looks at the floor in fear,
And love, as an act, lacks a verb; the zer-
o Euclid thought the vanishing point became
Wasn't math—it was the nothingness of Time.
    I sit by the window. And while I sit
    My youth comes back. Sometimes I'd smile. Or spit.

I said that the leaf may destroy the bud;
What's fertile falls in fallow soil—a dud;
That on the flat field, the unshadowed plain
Nature spills the seeds of trees in vain.
    I sit by the window. Hands lock my knees.
    My heavy shadow's my squat company.

My song was out of tune, my voice was cracked,
But at least no chorus can ever sing it back.
That talk like this reaps no reward bewilders
No one—no one's legs rest on my shoulders.
    I sit by the window in the dark. Like an express,
    The waves behind the wavelike curtain crash.

A loyal subject of these second-rate years,
I proudly admit that my finest ideas
Are second-rate, and may the future take them
As trophies of my struggle against suffocation.
    I sit in the dark. And it would be hard to figure out
    Which is worse: The dark inside, or the darkness out.

Howard Moss

Howard Moss is the poetry editor of *The New Yorker*. Before joining its staff in 1948, he was an instructor of English at Vassar College. The author of ten books of poems, including this one, and two books of criticism, *The Magic Lantern of Marcel Proust* and *Writing Against Time*, he has also edited the poems of Keats, the nonsense verse of Edward Lear, and a collection of short stories written by poets, *The Poet's Story*. A play, *The Folding Green*, was first produced by The Poets' Theater in Cambridge, Mass., and then by The Playwrights' Unit in New York City, and a more recent work, *The Palace at 4 A.M.,* was produced in the summer of 1972 at the John Drew Theater in East Hampton, with Edward Albee as its director. In the same year, Moss received the National Book Award for his *Selected Poems*. In 1974, he published a book of satirical biographies, *Instant Lives*, with drawings by Edward Gorey. Moss is a member of The National Institute of Arts and Letters and received a grant in creative writing from that organization in 1968.

Q3